Walking in Faith

TJ Dickson

Published by:

Taraji, LLC
P.O. Box 34131
Omaha, NE 68134

Copyright @ 2015 TJ Dickson
Photo by J. Bloom Photography
Edited by Breanna Carodine

Walking in Faith

First Edition
Printed and bound in the USA by Createspace, a DBA of On-Demand Publishing LLC, part of the Amazon group of companies.

For I know the plans I have for you, says the Lord. They are plans for good and not for disaster, to give you a future and a hope. ~ Jeremiah 29:11 NLT

Dedication

I dedicate this book to:

- God, My ALL, who has always been with me and keeps His promises not to leave nor forsake me and that He has good plans for me;

- My husband, who is one of the greatest gifts I have ever received. Your love, strength, and faith bless me daily. You are a great spirit who I love dearly;

- My children, who are the greatest blessings in my life. I am blessed and honored to be your mom. You motivate me to be my highest and best self. I love you all tremendously;

- My mother, who inspired me to seek healing of my mind, body, and spirit. I love you;

- My father, who always encouraged me to dream just like he did. He dreamed until the moment he took his last breath. Thank you Daddy for your love;

- My grandmother, whose values of education, pioneering, and determination still permeates throughout my family. She died before I could know her, but her values propel me to keep moving forward in my life. I am proud to be her granddaughter.

- My women's small group that offered me a place to share and receive support and resources to achieve my dreams. You ladies are godsend.

- My coaches, who were my accountability partners and cheerleaders to create and finish this book. Thank you so much for your service to me.

Contents

Forward...9

Writing These Books....................................11

Changing Positions.....................................13

Changing Careers.......................................17

Filing for Divorce.....................................19

Going to Church..23

Getting Married Again..................................25

Filing Bankruptcy......................................28

My Counselor...31

Healing the Kids.......................................35

Losing 50+ Pounds......................................37

He Talks to Me...40

Listening Daily for His Guidance.......................43

Contents

Forward

I was a little girl somewhere between first and third grade the first time I remember my faith was activated. I was a bookworm who worked hard in school and loved to play hard as well. I always looked forward to the annual school picnic where we would load the buses, go to a park, and have a day of fun. We would take an entire day to just play kickball, have bubblegum blowing contests, jump rope, run, and have a good time. Two years in a row our picnics were supposed to be rained out. I cried and prayed and pleaded to God to hold up the rain during our school day so we could go and have our picnic, and He did, both years! He listened to me and answered my prayer. He showed me that I mattered, that my prayers mattered, and that I had faith. I knew no one could make the rain stop but Him and I felt that if I sincerely asked, He might do it and He did! That was the cornerstone of my personal faith walk with God. And my faith has been building ever since.

Writing These Books

Today, I am being obedient. I am sitting in a coffee house writing on my lunch break—1 hour of uninterrupted writing time. Right now I don't know where these books will go or be used for exactly. I just write. This actually all started—the book that is—one night when I woke in the middle of the night with "titles" in my head. So, I wrote them down and did not know what more to do with them at the time. I just figured if I woke in the middle of the night, which is unlike me, these titles must mean something and God would give me the next step in His time and, eventually, He did. The next step took my mind back to high school to English class writing themes. Before you could write a theme after you chose the topic or had your "title", you had to prepare outlines. So, I took the titles and prepared outlines for each of them and several months later I am here each week taking myself to lunch to write and put the meat on the bones.

I write in a place that is calm, serene, inspiring, peaceful, and warm. The sunlight is shining on my back through the window of the coffeehouse. I have just polished off my chicken salad wrap and Lays Classic chips (my favorite!). Funny thing is I didn't order them they just so happened to come with the wrap. There are three colorful, paper butterflies hanging from the ceiling that I view as a sign from God. The butterfly is my symbol for transformation. God you are speaking to me! I am at the right place today to write. I am at peace and feeding my soul because I am letting out what is in it. I am initially handwriting this book. There is something about pen to paper that opens me up and feels good to me. Honestly, I don't know yet whether I am writing books or seminars, maybe both, but it matters not. I am simply open to whatever I am guided to do.

Changing Positions

I am a creature who tends to need to be kicked in the butt in order to move. This was no exception when I left my longest held position. I had been at that company for 7 years, 1 month, and 29 days. I had moved to the highest position in my chosen career field at the time.

The years at the former company were tolerable, at best, until one day all of the bullshit had gotten to be too much. I decided that I would have a new position by the end of that month. I sent out a great plea to God to move me to another organization or help me to suck it up but above all else, let His will be done and restore my peace. And He did just that.

My plea occurred after a nasty encounter with my supervisor right before I left the office to pick up my son from school. On the 10 minute drive, I cried. Work rarely makes me cry. When it does, a change is going to come. So, there I was in my car on the interstate sending out my plea, "God I don't know what your plans are, what you are trying to tell me. If you are telling me to seek employment elsewhere, I will do what you want. Perhaps, I am being a big baby now and I need to suck it up or maybe you are trying to get me to move. Just make it clear. And above all else, I want your will to be done and to have back my peace." Immediately, peace came over me and by the time I reached my son's school, my crying had ceased and I was calm. Later that night, I looked online at a career website and saw an opening at an organization that was a much higher position with more prestige and more money than I was making. So, I applied and I got it!

The hours for the position were perfect for me (early morning until late afternoon), and I felt like this was going to be my new place of employment. Prior to this interview, I prayed that I would get a sign through my spirit—a feeling of knowing if this was the new position and place of employment for me or not. Not only did I get it, it was as if they had been waiting for me. They had been looking for someone to fill the position and I was the perfect fit at the perfect time. Funny thing is during my first interview, one of the interviewers was a woman that my sister had spoken fondly of for years. I made it through the first interview with flying colors and then was asked back for a second.

The Executive Committee of the Board of Directors interviewed me. I was in a room full of men, who are executives and upper management of their perspective organizations, shooting questions at me from the left, the middle, and the right. They peppered me with questions for about an hour. By the time I left, I was a tad frazzled, but during the interview I was confident. I felt that I was a perfect fit. I had experience in working for nonprofits in the program and accounting areas, and I oversaw both operations and finance in the position I was leaving. I had the educational background with my business administration undergraduate and graduate degrees and an accounting major and emphasis. To top it off, I am from the community the organization primarily serves and I had run a program in a previous position that served the same community. Moreover, I was born and raised in the city and had seen the neighborhoods change over the years. I understood the fullness of the job and the issues being addressed by the organization.

Once my interview was over, I left the building and saw a woman I had met years before through my former spouse when she was his boss. She was delighted to see me. I thought she was just there for a meeting, and she was. But, I didn't know that she was the Secretary of the Board until she told me. She gave me a hug and said that everything was going to be alright and God is good. That was reassurance to me that the position was mine. God was giving me signs all along the way.

So, I got the position and was extended an offer to start immediately. My first day in my new position was my last day at my old one, September 30th. God honored my decision to be moved by the end of the month. My peace was restored.

Originally, I was going to stay in my former position until my son graduated in May and I could get my career in Wellness started lucratively. But, it became apparent that I had to switch positions before that time for my sanity and peace. Those two things were critical for me to move forward. So, now, here I am in my new position, my son has graduated, and now I am geared up ready for the next steps to my new career.

Changing Careers

I want to have a wellness center that includes services for the soul such as Reiki; massage; EMDR mental health therapy; nutrition; life coaching; fitness clubs focusing on walking, running, and biking, etc.; natural hair care; skincare; mani/pedis; makeup; financial wellness courses; meditation; life classes; speakers; book clubs; etc. My desire for this stems from the total revamp I went through to become who I am today, a happier, and healthier me. I sought out services and discovered many too. So, I think it would be great to put them all in one place to help others going through transformation.

Not only do I want to own such a center, I will coach, write, and speak in the wellness industry. I am a natural coach. I love to talk to people and encourage them. I empower them to win, and I love to see people win. I have done this for years with my kids and others in my life. I especially experienced it when I taught and supervised others. Writing these stories is another step to my career change.

When I coach, I feel passion and fulfillment and incredible energy surging through me. It is an amazing experience. I feel powerful and joyful when I coach. I look forward to coaching. When I write, I feel a release and hopeful. I have been writing since at least the 6th grade. I have written journals, poetry, and lesson plans. Now, I am an author in progress of writing my first book and telling my story! How awesome!

My faith is highly activated with this career change because I have been in the accounting industry for 25 years. I get hired because of my reputation and longevity in the industry. I am known as an accounting professional. It is what I have done. It is one of my four-year old self's dreams come true. Now, it is like I am starting over with this new career and industry. For now I will continue to take the steps that I am enlightened to take and will see where this goes.

Filing for Divorce

I met my former husband in 1988 when I was 18 years old. We dated for three and a half years, got married, bought two houses, and had three beautiful kids and two adorable dogs. We graduated five times between the two of us, started our careers, and built what appeared to be a nice, solid image of the middle class, professional, two-parent household. About 12 years ago my spirit realized that my marriage was over and I felt I had lost almost everything. I wanted to die. I headed towards a pillar as I was driving at a high rate of speed. In a moment of clarity I called out, "Jesus!" Then, my car straightened back out on the road and avoided hitting the pillar. It would take another four and a half years for my mind and body to get strong enough to accept that my marriage was over and start the process of divorce. I was desperate for love, for life, for air. I didn't know where to turn until I was lead to church.

For some people this would be a no-brainer, but for me, it was quite the opposite. I was not the "church type." I felt like I was a good person that tried to do good things. I didn't need to go to church with all of those "phony, not-nice people." Little did I know that the day I stepped foot into church my journey to spiritual health and wholeness would start.

Immediately, I felt love. After a while I began to

breathe again, and slowly, I started to live again. My relationship with God deepened. I learned that all I need comes from Him. He is love and gives love continuously and endlessly. He is breath and life. His plans for me are for good and not disaster and He works ALL things, no matter how bad they seem, to move me towards those plans.

Once my spiritual health was stronger, I then was led to work on my mental and emotional health. I initially started going to a Christian counselor because I didn't want my kids growing up with a bitter, mean, hateful mom. I was really concerned that I would turn into that kind of person because I had put so much into my marriage. I did everything I knew to do to have a successful marriage. I was not perfect, but I did try to be the best wife and mother I knew to be. I had a dream of being a successful wife and mom since I was four years old. To have that dream die was a MAJOR blow for me. So, the counseling sessions began. To my surprise and blessing all of my wounds, not just the ones from the marriage, but also ones from my childhood were exposed, dealt with, and healed. God is SO GOOD! If I had not gone through the divorce, I would have probably never dealt with my baggage. I am healthier, mentally and emotionally, than I can ever remember. I operate healthier in relationships than I ever have.

My physical health has also been affected. By 2009 I weighed the heaviest I had ever been. By 2011 I had lost 50 pounds and eight dress sizes. I felt and looked better! That year I completed my first ever half marathon and the next year I completed my first cycling challenge and second half marathon, beating my time from the prior year. Today, I am still active and started taking classes to learn new things like swimming, painting, Reiki, and belly dance. These classes have challenged and encouraged me to keep setting more goals. For example, I have a goal to complete a biathlon. In addition, these classes have helped me on my journey to health.

Classes like painting calm my spirit and bring me peace. When I was going through the hardest times, I got a vision of me at a canvas painting and it was peaceful, but weirdly I had never painted. I continually saw this same vision in my mind for a few years. So finally I took a painting class and discovered that I really am at peace and in a calm place when I paint. I get consumed with my painting and all of the stress seems to disappear. Painting offers me a healthy, creative outlet. Painting soothes my soul.

I also took Dave Ramsey's Financial Peace class in 2010, paid off my car, learned to properly budget; moved into a smaller, more manageable home; and started rebuilding my financial health. Since then, I have greater control over my money and spend it more wisely. I have also started a business focusing on health and wholeness, while I continue to work my job as I build it. Additionally, I became a facilitator for Dave Ramsey's Financial Peace so I could help others on their journey to health and wholeness!

Finally, I have found love again. God has blessed me with a man who has gone through a similar experience as I. He was also divorced with three minor children. Our children are similar ages with both of our sons being the youngest, except his son is much younger than mine. He is a great dad. He is loving, kind, positive, encouraging, and strong. He cares about how I feel and my needs. He is real. He is not perfect, nor does he expect me to be. He accepts me as I am. He wants the best for me. He is a praying man who believes in God. He doesn't read or talk about it; he simply is being about it. The man lives scripture; his life reflects that. We have a great time together and support each other's dreams. I believe we were put together to be a blessing to each other.

I dream again. I have joy again. I have God and I really need no one and nothing else. I know that He is blessing me with abundance. My health and wholeness is improving every day. I have faith that the better it gets the better it gets and I will consistently be enlightened to the next steps to living a healthy, fulfilled life.

Going to Church

I have attended and been a member of a Sabbath-keeping church since 2003. This year I decided to go to another church, a different denomination and a first day church. My daughter, son-in-law, sister, brother-in-law, sister-in-law, nieces, and nephew still attend the Sabbath-keeping church. My mother and two other children no longer attend and currently do not attend church. I had been a leader at the Sabbath-keeping church and was very involved until one of my sisters died in 2009. I felt tremendous stress and ballooned up to my highest weight ever. The church had several pastor changes since 2003 and the last few years experienced way too many for me. I started to feel like I would attend another church if they had Sabbath service.

One day I was at the Sabbath-keeping church and asked myself why I was there. My answer was "because people expect me to be there." It was not about God, my relationship with Him, or any spiritual growth. No. Instead, it was about not being talked about, other people's expectations, and routine. Well, that was not why I started going to church. I remember my son asked me when we first started going, how long was I going to attend. My answer was "when I get what I came to get," which was getting spiritually fed. I promised myself it would not be about the people because people can disappoint and turn me off. I told myself I would let NO ONE keep me from my spiritual food. So here I was at church, at a crossroads. I was no longer there for my intention. I was there being a people pleaser. So, I stopped going, but guilt hung over my head.

At the beginning of 2014, my husband and I started attending another church regularly. One day at the end of a sermon the pastor had us meditate and listen for God's voice. My spirit had been burdened by the guilt of me not attending the Sabbath-keeping church. After that meditation I felt peace. I felt that God would move me where He wanted me to be whether Sabbath-keeping or first day church or anywhere else for that matter. I felt that as long as I was growing and being fed, then I was honoring God and pleasing Him. By the end of that meditation the guilt was gone. I could relax and enjoy my new church home with my husband, a place where we could both be fed. I thank God for blessing us.

Getting Married Again...Discovering Other Centered Love

I am married again. This time to my wonderful keeper husband. He shows me other-centered love. This type of love I had not experienced. I had not been around too many people that loved me without it being about them, or having strings attached, or being abusive.

My husband has made me cry many times but not for being hurt by his actions. Instead, it was about him being kind to me with his actions. I remember a time when I went to his home for a date. I fell asleep on his couch. He did not get mad or annoyed at me. He brought out a blanket, covered me, and let me sleep. When I woke up I apologized profusely. He told me there was no need to apologize because I must have needed the sleep. He meant that sincerely and boy did that hit me. I wept. I did not expect such tenderness and understanding. It was of no benefit to him for me to sleep. If anything, I thought he would have at minimum, been angry because I did not stay awake to talk to him and watch a movie. But, none of that was important to him. My wellbeing was his only concern.

Wow, what a man! And he is my man! He is beautiful, loving, wise, and generous. God blessed me with him. He is not critical. He is very uplifting and full of wisdom. He loves people even when they do not love him back, but he is wise and will release relationships when they are toxic. He will give people chances and respect for more than sometimes I think they deserve.

He is a walking, living embodiment of using the Law of Attraction and applying the tenants of the Bible. He just seems to know the right thing to do particularly when it comes down to dealing with other people. His beliefs and his philosophies are so in line with truth. I wanted a man who I would really know and who was a follower of God. God granted me my desire with my husband.

He is strong in many ways. The man can pick me up, even when I weighed my heaviest of more than 200 pounds. Not only is he physically strong, he is emotionally and mentally strong. With all that he has gone through and all of the responsibility he has, he handles it like a trooper and a true gentleman. That takes much strength! I sometimes look at him in amazement when he keeps his cool under challenging circumstances.

He is brilliant, well-educated, and wise. He knows many things and yet is humble enough to realize that he does not know everything. When he is learning something new, he is so intent and respectful of the process. He likes to learn.

He is youthful, but not childish. He is a responsible person, who knows how to have fun. Whatever we do together is a blast! We like to try new cuisine, travel, go out in nature, discover new places, and attend events. He even likes to dance. I really like dancing and now I have a great dance partner.

Someone asked me what it feels like to be married. My answer: "natural." My relationship, the peace I am in now; it all feels so natural and yet mystical and spiritual. We have experienced so many coincidences in our relationship as it has naturally evolved. We have a lot in common. We even dress alike, but not on purpose. We like the same things—some of our favorite things have been our favorite things long before we ever met. We are so connected. He gets and appreciates me and I get and appreciate him. We are each other's best friend. It is so amazing, so awesome! We are blessed. I thank God for "do overs." And the best is yet to come!

Filing Bankruptcy

I was told by my mother when I was a little girl to take care of my money by paying my bills on time and taking care of my credit. I was so financially conscience that I prided myself on finding bargains and having nice things at a fraction of the price. I lived in a very nice house that my former spouse and I purchased at a bargain price and fixed up. My mother said that it looked like a home where two teachers should live; it was very impressive. It was a home that I believed we could have, so we got it. Looking back now I wonder if we just willed our way into that house.

In 2006 we put a large second mortgage on our home. I remember how I was very upset with my then spouse for wanting to do it and originally I refused to do it. Eventually I agreed but as I was sitting in the financial institution waiting to sign the papers, my intuition was screaming, "DON'T DO THIS!" I ignored it and signed the paperwork anyway. Later, that same intuition kicked in when my former spouse tried to get me to lease a new vehicle and this time I listened. Within months of these two occasions, my marriage was over.

I stayed in the house with the kids and paid the first mortgage while he paid the second. A time came when I would have to start paying the second mortgage as well as the first. I could not pay both. I tried to sell the house for more than two years. I fixed it up, maxed out my credit cards on repairs, and used at least three different agents, two of which were the best in the business and still I did not get an offer. So, while my credit was still good, I found home to rent and immediately filed bankruptcy. It was a tough decision for me. I had paid my bills on time, paid who I owed, watched my spending, and supported a decision my then-spouse made. However, when it came down to having money for food or pay two mortgages, I chose food.

I was so angry at my former spouse but even more so with myself. God warned me not to sign those papers and I ignored it and chose my former spouse's wants over what I knew better to do. I could only really blame myself. Thank God I listened about the vehicle though because I ended up losing my house, but not my car. I had chosen to purchase a used Honda instead of leasing a new vehicle. This car was reliable and served me well along with my daughter and her husband. They both drove it debt-free. That car was a tremendous blessing and ran over 200,000 miles.

When you listen, God's way is best. Even when you refuse, God still can take your mess ups and turn them into triumph. Since that experience, I have been very careful to not get into debt like that again. I have a written cash flow statement and strive to pay cash as much as possible. I was also blessed with losing that house. It continually required repairs until I finally let it go. Renting a home was a new experience for me, but after dealing with that overwhelming home I owned, renting was a relief. The home was manageable. I rested in that home. Boy, did I need it! I stayed in that house until my keeper husband and I got a house together.

Now, I live in the biggest, grandest home I have ever lived. I love my master suite where I can go to and rest. This house has enough room for us to all spread out and have private space if needed. God took the bankruptcy and turned it into good. More importantly, He took away the shame. I no longer have guilt for filing bankruptcy and letting go of the house. Funny thing is someone purchased the home almost immediately after I let it go. They rented it out to a large family who needed the space. That house has been a blessing for the owners and the tenants plus the financial institution recouped some of its money as well. Things always work out. Thank you God!

My Counselor

I prayed for my counselor. I lay spread across a desk one day in October 2007 completely distraught. I prayed that God would allow me to discover a Christian counselor and I needed to see that person that same day. I could no longer wait. So, I searched online and found two names—the first person could not see me that day. I left a message at the second person's office and received a call back shortly after stating that he could see me that day. Immediately, I felt hope and got up and proceeded to do my work. I arrived at my appointment that afternoon and met my counselor for the first time, an older, tough-as-nails, turned pastor and counselor later in life, guy who pastors and counsels with his wife. I knew God had sent this man. I did not question our many differences, because I just knew God was in it. Breakthroughs occurred the first session and they continued to occur for the next two years that I regularly saw him.

He always started each session with a prayer and asked for God's power and wisdom. He said that God was the Ultimate Counselor. This made me feel so assured that healing was going to take place in the session. I also did my part and asked and believed God for breakthroughs even on days when I walked in and intellectually and emotionally, did not know what specific area needed healing. I experienced healing with those sessions and the healing was powerful! Deep wounds, old wounds, multiple wounds, festering wounds were healed.

The reason I went to him in the first place was to prevent me from being bitter because of my failed relationship. I had not yet gone through divorce, but I knew that it was going to happen and I wanted to go through and live after it with as much grace as possible. I knew that my children would have enough to deal with, with the divorce and I needed to be in as positive and strong space as possible to not add to their pain. Not only did I not become bitter, I got better!

I was healed of wounds from the marriage, the divorce, and from childhood. I got better than I was before and let go of things I had held onto. For instance, I was extremely cautious of anyone caring for my children other than me so daycare was not an option. I went to a daycare when I was about two or three years old that I was petrified to attend. It wasn't just a strong dislike of it or separation anxiety. I was so fearful of that place that I would freeze when I would arrive. My mom would have to literally peel my fingers off the car door and bend my body for me to get into the house. I knew that there was something that had really went wrong at that daycare. As a result, I promised myself I would never put my kids in daycare. I would take care of my children myself no matter the sacrifice. I also would not let the kids go over other people's houses and definitely not spend the night. I told my counselor about this memory and he took me back to the memory while using EMDR. I was able to remember more. I witnessed something there that terrified me. I could not fully remember, however. But, it was enough. I was healed so that I started to release the gripping fear I had to protect my children. I know that helped my children develop better and live healthier lives. I also released a lot of anger and sadness from other childhood memories. I have become the healthiest I have been in my memory. I am embracing myself and loving me for me.

My counselor also helped me to understand my wonderful keeper husband and how he loves me. He told me that his love was other-centered which I did not understand because I had not experienced it before. I had to rewire my brain to understand healthy loving relationships. My counselor also taught me to respond in a way which is appropriate. That has been invaluable to me to stay healthy.

The day I got married again, I walked into my counselor's office for what might be the last time. So many days I had walked in to see him when I was in so much pain, unhappy, and sad, but not this day. On this day I walked in and asked my counselor to put on his pastor hat to officiate my wedding ceremony. I was joyful, happy, and ecstatic. I was marrying my love. God is good! I had come full circle from seeking help through my divorce to celebrate finding true love. My counselor had been through it all and I thank God for him.

Healing the Kids

Since the moments I knew I was pregnant with my children, I knew they were special. God had called me to be their mom. My thoughts were to provide them the best environment I could for them to grow and develop their wings to fly. I feel like a mama bird right about now pushing her babies out of the nest and watching them take flight.

When my divorce happened, it was brutal. My kids really suffered. A family member told me they would not make it because I was divorcing their dad. That was the cruelest thing I could be told, but the devil is a lie. I made it my duty as their mom to empower them to make it. God said they would make it and I knew that God called them for a purpose. Though I was not sure of the purpose, I knew they had it. I dug my heels in and held on really tight, stood, fought, prayed, expected, kept the faith, and demanded that they make it. And they did! Yes Lord!

The kids all showed signs of trauma so they all went to counseling. I drew boundaries. They made mistakes and violated some of my rules, but that was okay because I understood and loved them anyway. I made mistakes and violated some of my own rules and that was okay too because I understood and loved me anyway. I loved all of us in our imperfections. I judged less and loved more. The time was healing because the standards were not more important than the people; the people were the most important. Some days I did not know what to do but God did. He helped me through the pain of seeing them in pain. He protected them even through tough situations. He led them through mistreatment and toxicity. He sent them people who mentored them and played the confidante, had fun with them, and loved and cared for them when those who they relied on failed them. He sent a village to help me raise my kids. For that, I am incredibly grateful.

He also sent our two little dogs to love the kids and me and comfort us through it all. The dogs are incredible. They always knew which child needed them most and on which days. The dogs brought healing, comfort, laughter, fun, and love to them especially in their darkest moments.

He sent opportunities for empowerment and to do work they love and they are called to do. My oldest was called to do pageantry and social work, my middle was called to work with children, and my youngest had the opportunity to participate in some information technology internships. God gave them what they needed to still fly in spite of the divorce. They received scholarships, financial aid, and grants for college. They are giving back to this world the awesomeness that is them. They are flying!

Losing 50+ Pounds

I started my journey to lose weight when I had an "ah-ha" moment in the fall of 2009 when I weighed my heaviest. I was sedentary mostly. My job required me to sit hours on end. During that time, my sister had been sick and died. Plus, I had a child who had been hospitalized. I was making up time at work which caused me to work 11 and 12 hour days sitting majority of the time. I would eat at my desk so I would not have to use hours for lunch breaks. During the ten minute breaks I would go pick up food from the restaurant in our complex. One day in December I was going to pick up my lunch and was walking up the stairs outside. It was snowy out, but the stairs were completely clear and were not steep. A guy was outside watching and as I came up the stairs I nearly fell. He thought I had slipped on ice, but my legs gave out under my weight. I stumbled and caught myself. I could not believe what I had experienced. I was only 39 at the time and I had let myself get that out of shape. That was a wake -up call for me.

I started a workout plan and lost 13.5 pounds by March of the following year and kept off 10. While on the plan, I felt that something was still off. I ate healthy food, but I still felt like I was not eating right. Then, life happened. I stopped working out because I did not think I had the time. My oldest graduated high school and won a pageant. I had to travel, host parties and go to her appearances. Although all of that was great, my body and mind were telling me to invest in myself and get healthier.

One day I was sitting at my desk thinking about my grandmother. My mother talked about how she would sit at her sewing machine for hours upon hours. It seemed that my grandmother worked herself to death and did not take care of herself. So, there I was at the desk and all of sudden the thought came over me, "She killed herself sitting at her machine and you are killing yourself sitting at this desk." That shook me. Within days I joined a weight loss program.

I went from nearly falling from my big legs buckling under me to being able to run, dance, workout, and complete three half marathons along with numerous other smaller races. I learned so much about my body, about portion control, and how to eat to live instead of living to eat. I learned how not to eat my emotions away by using my words instead of stuffing them back down my throat with food. I felt so much better and empowered to create health in every area of my life.

In 2012, I wrote the following poem regarding my relationship with food:

I Eat Because...

I eat to live.
I eat to hide.
I eat to drown.
I eat to comfort.
I eat to fill.
I eat to avoid.
I eat to celebrate.

I eat my peace.
I eat my joy.
I eat my opportunities.
I eat my goals.
I eat my accomplishments.
I eat my emptiness.
I eat my growth.

Too much eating.

If hunger isn't the problem, then food is not the answer!

STOP!

He Talks to Me

In 2012 I discovered meditation when I decided to get certified as a Law of Attraction coach. Studying Law of Attraction gave me pause because I was concerned about it conflicting with my religion. As part of the course, I learned to meditate. Then, I learned that in the Bible there is meditation: "Be still and know that I am God." Psalms 46:10. "Meditate on the word day and night." Joshua 1:8. Meditation has enhanced my faith. See to me prayer is when you ask and talk to God. Whereas, meditation is when you listen and God talks to you. For years I just talked and it was a one-sided conversation.

In the beginning I was concerned whether I was meditating correctly and if I was really hearing God or if it was just my thoughts. I learned quickly that God is with me ALL THE TIME and I can tap in any time I want. He is right here. So, daily I meditate. I ask God questions and he answers. I read a book called, *The Man Who Talks to the Flowers*, a story about George Washington Carver. Mr. Carver went into the woods every morning to ask God what he was to do in that day.

The messages I received most from the story were that George found God in nature. He loved flowers and he found God in them. He expected them to reveal their secrets to him as result. He believed that if you love anything enough, it will reveal its secrets to you. Love, humility, and expectation lead to the doorway to God and sometimes, man's disappointments leads to God's appointment. George Washington Carver became known as one of history's greatest scientists and we still enjoy his discoveries today.

God speaks to me in other ways too. He communicates with me through spoken words, written words, my urges, inklings, feelings, intuition and He fulfills my intentions. For example, I had been praying to hear God's voice and be lead by Him. One day I received an email regarding people being like sheep that we hear God's voice and He leads us. That email reassured me that I was on the right track.

I too walk in nature. I call it my time with God. When I walk, things become clear. My mind releases what no longer serves me. I get messages that propel me forward, soothe me, and comfort my soul. I learn from nature about faith. Like in Matthew 6:26-30, "Look at the birds. They don't need to plant or harvest or put food in barns..." That is so true. Nature calms me, energizes me, and builds my faith in God. I see Him in nature, in the little ones, in people. He lives.

I also learned about guided meditation while I was a Law of Attraction coaching student. Those meditations were an excellent way for me to make discoveries about myself. To get quiet and really tap into the person I am authentically.

God used those meditations to help me to forgive, discover wisdom within me, and envision the great future that lies ahead of me. I reclaimed parts of myself, my emotions, and my soul that were left in former toxic, painful relationships that ended. By reclaiming those pieces, I healed and therefore built healthier relationships. I felt better, whole, and eager. For me those meditations helped me to take a much needed break for my soul to rest and be healed even if it was for only 10 minutes.

Meditation for me has been invaluable whether done by being alone in my closet, bathroom, taking a walk among the trees, or going through guided meditation focusing on a specific purpose. All have served to heal my spirit, draw me closer to God, and increase my faith. For this I say, "Thank You God!"

Listening Daily for His Guidance

During my course to become a Law of Attraction coach, I started a Law of Attraction journal. Daily I would write down what I would intend for the day, what I am grateful for, my prayer, and my meditation. Recently, I added a Bible passage. (Prior to this I completed a journey to read the entire Bible as part of my healing and spiritual growth.) I have used this journal to focus my thoughts on goodness, my desires, abundance, gratefulness, God's messages directly to me, and His Word. This practice has become one of the greatest things I have done to increase my faith and keep my mind and thoughts on God's goodness. When I reread my journals and see all that has manifested and the blessings of God even in the matters that felt painful or scary, I see that ALL things work together for good for those who love the Lord.

I have used the journal to set up my days so that I start them focused, my energy is aligned, my intentions and gratitude are expressed, I have talked to God and He has talked to me letting me know what He wants me to know for that day. God is so amazing! I thank Him for expansion of my spiritual walk and journey with Him. Now, I not only talk to Him, I listen too! I cannot emphasize that enough—Listen. He has so many powerful, invaluable things to convey. He told me to not let anyone judge me for going to a new church because He sent me there, to forgive and release those with whom I had broken relationships, that my children would make it, that my new home would be spectacular, to write, and the list could go on and on.

I have never and will never be alone because God always has and always will be with me! I thank God for my growing faith in Him. I have prayed and still pray for continued growth and abundance of faith. My prayer is being answered. I am learning, growing, and continually experiencing evidence of faith. Indeed, I am walking in faith. Thank You Father!

www.ingramcontent.com/pod-product-compliance
Lightning Source LLC
Chambersburg PA
CBHW051713090426

42736CB00013B/2685